The Red Dragon

I fy mhlant annwyl a chall
Elliw, Gwenno ac Owain
ac i fy rhieni, Alan a Catherine
– cenedlaetholwyr cadarn, pobl dda
a rhieni gwerthfawr

The Red Dragon

Dragon

The story of the Welsh Flag

Siôn T.Jobbins

yLolfa

Dragon passant in stained glass at Hammond Castle; photo by Stu Horvath

First published: 2016

© Siôn T. Jobbins & Y Lolfa Cyf., 2016

Book and cover design: Y Lolfa
Cover photograph: M.Dunham/AP/Sipa
ISBN: 978-1-78461-135-4

Published and printed in Wales
on paper from well managed forests
by Y Lolfa Cyf., Talybont, Ceredigion SY24 5HE
e-mail ylolfa@ylolfa.com
website www.ylolfa.com
tel 01970 832 304
fax 832 782

Introduction

There are many things we Welsh aren't too clever at.

Although our food produce is of excellent quality, our traditional cuisine is not known for being the most tasty or innovative. Our towns and villages are mostly accidental sprawls without centres or civic squares. We're not known for our flair; in fact, we're hardly known at all. Our heroism in battle is in fighting for the freedom of other nations and not our own.

But we can be very proud of our flag.

The Red Dragon flag emanates a kind of Welsh genius which occasionally, very occasionally, peeks out as a rare ray of warm sunshine behind the grey cloud of Welsh mediocrity and shrugging acceptance.

Its genius, like that of our anthem, is that it can belong to everyone.

It is not a narrow political flag like those of Communist China or Vietnam, national flags which are associated with particular parties. It has not been changed repeatedly by different partisan governments, like Georgia's in the Caucuses.

It is neither republican nor monarchist and so avoids the kind of difficulty which other nations face: for example, the bloody symbolism associated with the white Bourbon flag of the French monarchy and the republican French tricolour.

It's not a flag born or baptised in the blood and

denigration of other peoples, like the Union Jack, Soviet Union, and old South Africa. Its success is not that it causes fear or dread for others, but that it gives its own people innocent happiness.

It is neither too English or British for those who wish an independent Welsh identity, nor too closely associated with Welsh nationalism for those who don't.

Surprisingly, for the flag of a nation which has such a long and proud Christian tradition, our flag doesn't include any Christian symbolism such as a cross. It thus causes no offence, intentional or imagined, for those who have no Christian faith.

Its design is so striking that it is remembered and recognised by anyone who sees it, however fleetingly. Not for us the easy-to-confuse designs of less fortunate peoples – nations whose flags are damned to being mistaken at official ceremonies. I'm looking at you, Slovenia and Slovakia; all pan-Arab, pan-African and former Bolivarian republic flags! And whilst we're at it, having a simple design is crucial for any flag, but hey, Indonesia, make an effort!

The Red Dragon does have one design mistake which we should admit to. The lower half of the Red Dragon, by overlapping the green, breaks the design rules of tincture and so can't be seen clearly from a distance. However, this is a small blip compared to more serious design crimes such as Bangladesh's, with their red sun on green background, all seen as brown by colour-blind people.

And, thank heavens, the flag wasn't designed by a committee or voted for in a competition or referendum.

It is a flag whose central design, the Dragon, is among the oldest continuously-used national icons found on any of the world's national flags. The only other challenge to its record-breaking longevity would come from Bhutan's flag – also featuring a dragon.

Despite its roots in the era of spears and woad, the flag was officially accepted only in clean-shaven 1959. The Red Dragon, not coincidentally, came of age at the time of the anti-colonial 'wind of change' sweeping Africa and the other colonised peoples of the British Empire.

Within the design and history of the Red Dragon flag is the history and the psychology of the Welsh people. It's the profile we'd like to present to others and the way we'd like to think of ourselves. The flag – its struggle to be invented, recognised and used – says a lot about the *chaise longue* of psychological neurosis which is the Welsh nation.

For every flag is a book. The colours and design have all been chosen and fought for. The success, beauty and danger of flags are that they encapsulate very complex ideas, identities, history and ambition in one simple piece of cloth. To know the history of a country's flag is to know the history of the people who fly it. In fact, it is to know a more nuanced and hidden history of that nation than many of the flag-flyers are unaware of.

Read on – and then, and when you see the Red Dragon flag (and how can you miss it in Wales?) you will not only 'see' a three-coloured flag, but will also be able to 'read' it.

The Red Dragon of Wales, *Y Ddraig Goch*, is a good flag. Fly it high and fly it often.

Beginnings – the Dragon's Tongue

The Welsh language is the oldest continuously spoken language of the island of Britain. It has seen off Latin, Norman-French and precedes Anglo-Saxon and English.

What Latin is to Italian, Brythonic is to Welsh. Brythonic (one could call it Ancient Welsh: after all, we say 'Ancient Greek') was related to the Celtic languages of Gaul (present day France) and also Goidelic, which became Irish and Scots Gaelic and Manx.

Brythonic was spoken across the whole of what is today southern Scotland, England and of course Wales.

With the advance of the Anglo-Saxons during the anarchy following the withdrawal of the Romans in the fifth century, the Brythonic lands were split. Wales was cut off from the Welsh in what is known as '*yr Hen Ogledd*' in Welsh (the Old North) after the battle of Chester in 615 AD and the Welsh in what is now south-west England at the battle of Dyrham in 577. The earliest Welsh poetry was composed not in Wales but in the Old North, includes the poetry of Taliesin, and records the lost kingdoms of Rhedeg and Elmet and of tribes such as the Gododdin.

Welsh names are like graffiti on the map of England and Scotland – the city of Perth in Scotland means 'bush', Partick in Glasgow means '*perthog*' (bushy); Dover in England is from the old Welsh '*dwfr*' ('*dŵr*' in modern

Welsh flags at the National Eisteddfod; photo by Roger Lloyd Williams

Welsh – water), and 'Avon' the river and county, means, simply 'river' ('*afon*' in Welsh).

The Brythons were hemmed into Wales and Cornwall, where the language diverged into Welsh and Cornish. Some Brythons fled from the invading Anglo-Saxons to Brittany and the language evolved, possibly with the earlier Celtic Gaulish language, into Breton, Welsh's other sister language.

Split from the Brythons in '*yr Hen Ogledd*' and from the Cornish in the south, by the ninth century the Brythons in the two central wet and windy western peninsulas began to call themselves *Combrogi*, from the words *com* (co) and *brog* (land), which means, essentially compatriots. Over time the word became 'Cymru' for the country and 'Cymry' for Welsh people. They are pronounced the same. 'Cumbria' in England retains the older version of the word.

The English word for us is 'Welsh'. It is from the Anglo-Saxon, '*walha*', and means 'Romanised foreigners'. It is essentially the same word as those used for other Romanised foreigners who inhabit the border of the Germanic-speaking world: these include the French-speaking Walloons in Belgium and Wallachia in Romania. 'Welsch' is still a term used in some German dialects for Italians in much the same way as 'wop' is in English.

Why do I say this? Well, because it helps explain why a dragon became our symbol.

The Welsh saw themselves as the original people and rightful owners of what we today call England. The Welsh also saw themselves as the inheritors in this island to the glory of Roman civilisation and of the Christian faith which was under threat by the pagans from the east.

Brythonic was greatly influenced by Latin, both grammatically and in vocabulary: not only in words for new concepts which may have arrived with the Romans, like '*ffenestr*' (window), '*pont*' (bridge), '*llyfr*' (book), but even words like '*lleidr*' (thief), '*braich*' (arm) or '*mur*' (wall), which Celtic would surely have had words for. This Latin influence helps explain the difference from Irish, our cousin Celtic language. It's not hard to imagine that another three generations of Roman rule and Brythonic may have died, to be replaced by Latin. Who knows? Today Wales could be speaking a Romance language similar to French or Spanish but with a heavy Celtic influence.

Unless one believes in history and culture being based on blood and ethnicity, the Welsh language is the one direct, unbroken link between us and our Celtic past and Roman memory. It is through that language that a sense of separateness and history has been passed on. But it is through the Red Dragon flag that people of all backgrounds can access and connect to that history. That's why the Red Dragon flag is such a powerful and unifying symbol.

The Age of Dragons

And so, we come to dragons.

Dragons and serpent-like creatures inhabit the imagination of communities across the globe. They appear in the arts and artefacts of ancient Babylonian, Persia, India and China. It seems that every civilization has attached an importance to dragons, which makes it even more surprising that it is only Wales (and Bhutan) which have placed them on their flags.

The Welsh word '*draig*' and English 'dragon' come, through Latin, from the Greek '*drakôn*' which means 'to see afar', or 'strong sighted', and could represent the gods of light or the heavens.

Dragons appear in many European cultures and mythologies. Slavic mythology describe змей (*smey* or words cognate to it), a four-legged beast which devours maidens and threatens villages. The Slavic dragon could have seven heads. The Basque Herensuge flew leaving a trail of fire and making a terrifying sound.

Norse and Germanic mythology are full of dragons including Níðhöggr which gnaws at the root of the world-tree, or Jörmungandr the sea-serpent, which surrounds the world or mortal men.

In Christianity the 'great red dragon' in the Book of Revelation is the sign of Satan, but it seems that its symbol of strength was more potent that its association with evil. But then, of course, is it not better to have a mighty, though evil, dragon defend you, than to be vanquished by your enemy?

It is only in Welsh mythology that the dragon is so consistently seen as a force of good (for the Welsh, at least). Among all the European nations, despite their long acquaintance with dragons, only Wales has continuously identified with it over the course of at least 1,500 years.

Why is this?

Because of the Welsh folk memory of the Roman Empire.

Roman Dragons

In Latin, a '*draco*' was a cohort of soldiers, between 300 and 600 in number. Ten dracos made a legion in the Roman army. Flying the dragon became the cohort's standard, and the standard-bearer was called a '*draconarius*'. The legion would carry an eagle standard.

It's not certain from whom the Romans adopted this tradition – maybe from the Dacians or Parthians of the Balkans or even the Scythians of the windy steppes above the north Black Sea coast. The Romans carried these dragon pennants into battle and there are twenty dragon standards carved on Trajan's Column in Rome (106 AD) and on the Arch of Galerius (311 AD).

The historian Ammianus Marcellinus describes the entry of Constantius into Rome in 357 AD 'surrounded by dracones, woven out of purple [*purpureus*] thread and bound to the golden and jewelled tops of spears, with wide mouths open to the breeze and hence hissing as if roused by anger, and leaving their tails winding in the wind'.

The colour and splendour of the dragons flying in the wind must have been an impressive sight in battle or parade. The sinister, continuous hissing sounds would have unnerved opponents in the same way as the Zulu's *uSuthu* war chant at Rorke's Drift, where the South Wales Borderers awaited the onslaught.

As the Latin word '*purpureus*' can mean a continuum of colours from red to almost black it's possible that many of these dragons would have been of a reddish colour. If the heads of these dragon pennants were made of bronze, then a polished bronze with its orange hue could also have been referred to as '*coch*'.

The dragon pennant was adopted by the Byzantines, Carolingians, Vandals and Saxons and Vikings. Maybe the question we should ask is not why the dragon is the symbol of Wales, but why is it not today the symbol of a Scandinavian or a Slavic nation?

Does our very own language – the unbroken link to the Roman period – contain an answer? Perhaps.

'*Draig Goch*' is in fact two Latin words '*draco coccinus*'. We already know the word for dragon came to Welsh from Latin, but '*coch*', the Welsh word for red, is also from Latin from a word for scarlet, '*coccinus*', which again, came originally from Greek. This was a Vulgar Latin (spoken Latin) of the late Roman period and lives on in the Albanian word for red too, 'kuq' and in Modern Greek as κόκκινος (kokkinos).

There is another, less-used word for red in Welsh,

'*rhudd*', which shares the same ancient root as the English, German or French words (red, *Rot* or *rouge*) and is also used in the other Celtic languages, '*ruzh*' in Cornish and Breton, '*rua*' in Irish. It can be found in Welsh words like '*llofrudd*' the word for murderer, which is made of two words, '*llof*' – the old form of hand; and '*rhudd*' red – that is, red (blood) hand.

Did the Roman *draconarius* chatting up the Brythonic native girls in a damp Caerleon or a busy Cirencester street, refer to the '*draco coccinus*'? Was this a specific red, and is its specific resonance one reason why this word for red, unique in Western European languages, is used, rather than the common and older '*rhudd*'? Is the very word '*coch*' some melancholic *hiraeth* for the splendour of a greater past?

We can imagine that the Latin '*draco coccius*' became Brythonic '*draca coca*'. Like the Latin word '*furca*' (fork) became '*fforch*' in Welsh, the 'c' sound changed to 'ch'. So Brythonic may have said '*draca cocha*', with the final 'a' showing that '*draca*' is a feminine word. As Brythonic developed into Welsh the loss of the word endings and standardising mutation '*Draig Coch*' became '*Draig Goch*'. The 'c' mutates to 'g' to signify that '*draig*', too, is feminine. The word '*draig*' is further also mutated if it's after the definite article, '*y*' (the), because '*draig*' is feminine. And so, two Latin words become Welsh.

End of Empire

As the Roman Empire collapsed, the Brythonic lands were attacked from the east by the Anglo-Saxons and from the west by the Irish. Arthurian myths are from this period (not the Middle Ages of English propaganda), and deal with the efforts of the embattled Brythons to keep the unity of Romano-Brythonic Britain from the invading Anglo-Saxons and civil war.

It is no surprise, then, that '*draig*' in Welsh came to mean 'soldier' as well as dragon? Uther Pendragon, Arthur's father, could be Uther 'Chief Dragon' or 'Chief Soldier' ('*pen*' being Welsh for head or, in this case, chief).

The link with the Romans may explain why the Welsh held on to the Dragon, but other Germanic people unconquered by the Romans, didn't. But why then isn't the Dragon the symbol of the Italians – they are, after all, the direct heirs to the Roman legions?

Was it because the Roman association and Celtic mythology combined in a heady brew?

In one tradition (recalled by the twelfth-century chronicler, Geoffrey of Monmouth) Uther, on the death of his brother, who was King of Britain, saw an incredible star in a vision. From this star there followed a 'ball of fire emanating from the figure of a dragon'. When Uther consulted Myrddin (Merlin the Magician) he was told that the meaning of the flaming dragon was that he, Uther, would be king of Britain. Uther had two golden dragons made, and demanded that one was kept at the Diocese of Winton and the other by himself to be 'taken into battle'. The dragon had become a solid object.

Uther's son, Arthur, inherited the dragon, and in his battle with the Roman Emperor, Lucius, he raised the dragon golden standard so that those who were wounded and tired could go to it to recover. This is a myth, of course, but here we see the dragon – symbol of fear and danger in other traditions – mutating into a Welsh symbol of comfort and defence.

Cadwaladr ap Cadwallon was, by tradition, the last Brythonic king of ancient Britain. He reigned at the time of two the great plagues (in 664 and 682), which hit the indigenous Brythonic population and gave the Anglo-Saxons time to conquer in the greatly depopulated land in England. He did battle with the English, but renounced his throne in 688 to become a pilgrim to Rome, in response to a prophecy that his sacrifice would bring about a future final victory of the Britons over the Anglo-Saxons and restore the land to the indigenous people. For this Christian deed he was known as Cadwaladr Fendigaid (Cadwaladr the Blessed). The Red Dragon became associated with Cadwaladr, and 800 years later a certain Henry Tudor claimed descent from Cadwaladr in his effort to claim legitimacy to the English throne.

The earliest written source of the Red Dragon as a Welsh symbol comes in the work of the Welshman Nennius in the early ninth century. The book includes traditions which go back to the seventh century or even earlier. Nennius's story was later recalled and adapted by Geoffrey of Monmouth in the twelfth century.

Lludd and Llefelys were mythical brothers, and the kings of Britain and of France respectively. A series of plagues engulfed the Isle of Britain, where the second plague was a terrifying scream. Lludd asked his brother for help and advice. Llefelys told him that the shrieks were those of a dragon being attacked by a foreign dragon. The only way to rid the land of the dragons was to dig a huge pit and place a cauldron of mead in it, into which the two dragons would fall, drink the mead and fall asleep. Lludd followed the advice and successfully buried the dragons in Snowdonia.

Years later, Gwrtheyrn (Vortigern in Latin) attempted to build a castle in Snowdonia. (In another story, Gwrtheyrn is blamed for letting in the English into Britain by giving the Isle of Thanet in Kent to the Anglo-Saxons Hengist and Horsa). In this story, Gwrtheyrn could never finish building the castle at Dinas Emrys (near today's Beddgelert in Gwynedd) as every night the castle walls were torn down. The walls fell because beneath the mountain two dragons, one red and the other white, were fighting.

Gwrtheyrn is advised to find a boy without a father and sprinkle the castle walls with his blood. The boy is found; in later versions of the tale he is named as Myrddin. He tells Gwrtheyrn to dig a hole into the mountain to release the fighting dragons. The dragons fly out and continue to fight. Although the white dragon is initially stronger, it is ultimately the Red Dragon which overcomes and drives the White Dragon away. Myrddin deciphers the battle as a battle between the Welsh Red and the English White Dragon, and that the Welsh will drive the English back across the sea and reclaim Britain.

As Dr Evelien Bracke notes, there are many elements to this mythology which are common to other European

A contemporary English white dragon

traditions – dragons fighting in the sky; drugging dragons with alcohol and imprisoning them; and locating them in desolate and mountainous areas. However, what is unique to the Welsh story is that the dragons are released.

No doubt the Christian religion, where the dragon is equated with the devil would have encouraged many nations not to have a positive image of dragons. This makes it even more surprising that the Welsh should embrace the Dragon. After all, the Brythons adopted Christianity at the end of the Roman period and despised the paganism of the Anglo-Saxons. The works of the ancient Welsh mythology, the Mabinogi, have been heavily adapted and censored to conform to Christian sensibilities, so the Welsh were sensitive to Christian norms and world-view. Attachment to this dragon must have been a deep tradition.

Only in Wales and the Far East are dragons associated

with wealth and power, such as in the Chinese New Year celebrations.

But maybe we talk too much of mythology. At the time of Nennius and later, we should remember that the Welsh *and* the English carried dragons into battle. The English kingdom of Wessex flew the golden or sometimes white dragon. The Welsh would have been familiar therefore with red and white dragons fighting each other, not only in mythology but on the bloodied battle field itself.

The Welsh liked their dragons and it seems, the dragons liked and favoured the Welsh. Remember: no Welshman ever killed a dragon.

Icon of King Cadwaladr at the Orthodox church of the Holy Protection, Blaenau Ffestiniog, based on a stained glass image c.1500 at Eglwys Llangadwaladr, Ynys Môn (Anglesey)

The Age of Princes and the Age of Gentry

The period from about the beginning of the eleventh century to the death of Prince Llywelyn in 1282 is known in Welsh as '*Oes y Tywysogion*' (the Age of Princes). From 1282 until around the end of the sixteenth century is '*Oes yr Uchelwyr*' (the Age of the Gentry). It was the princes, and then the gentry, who sponsored the Welsh poets. It is from their poetry, often written in wonderful, intricate, alliterating poetic meter (*cynghanedd*) that we learn so much of Welsh life.

By the eleventh century the border between Wales and England, was quite defined along Offa's Dyke, though Welsh was spoken on both sides. The border was porous and could change and battles and skirmishes were common. This was true of the use of the dragon too. But, as we know, there was also an English tradition of dragons or wyverns.

Following the Norman invasion the dragon standard was adopted by the conquerors. In 1138 it was the Scottish royal standard. Richard I (the Lionheart) took a dragon standard to the Third Crusade in 1191.

The dragon proved less fortunate for Henry III and the English army at the battle of Lewes in 1216. However, he installed the dragon standard at Westminster Abbey, and it was used by his son Edward I. The English king Henry III took the Red Dragon into battle against the

Welsh in Snowdonia in 1245. It was, perhaps, a way of disheartening the Welsh by saying that he came as the inheritor of the Brythonic rulers of Britain.

It was with the cult of St George which swept into England from the Crusades, and the image of the saint killing the dragon that the English gradually stopped using the dragon. St George could become an English patron saint as he was identified as killing Satan. And in an age of war with the Welsh, a dragon-slaying saint would have been an obvious and powerful propaganda tool and one to appeal to English patriotism. The dragon-slayer was a Welsh-slayer too. But the dragon didn't disappear completely from English use. It was flown by Edward III at the battle of Crécy (1346).

In a readable but rather passive-aggressive attitude towards the Celtic nations, Nick Groom notes in his *The Union Jack: the Story of the British Flag* that not one Welsh royal or gentry crest includes a red dragon. However, the dragon, it seems was above individual royalty or gentry as it was the symbol of the Welsh nation. That is, despite the recent fashion of discussing nations as abstract and imagined communities, the Welsh had a very strong and clear sense of themselves in the middle ages.

And it is here that we may ponder the lack of Welsh participation in the Crusades and our flag's story.

Despite Gerald of Wales's famous tours of Wales to rally soldiers for the Crusades, very few Welshmen actually made the journey to regain the Holy Land for Christianity from the Muslims. The made their excuses and stayed at home. And whilst the English Crown was away fighting a foreign 'just war' (a tradition it still maintains), the Welsh, when not fighting each another, consolidated their land and nationality.

The Crusades, as Grahame Davies notes in his book *The Dragon and the Crescent*, gave the Welsh a century or so breathing space to solidify their institutions, language and society. It's once the Crusades are over, or rather once Edward I stops crusading, that the '*Drang nach Westen*' begins again against the Welsh. Without that century or so of relative respite, there may now not be a Welsh nation at all.

Had the Welsh rallied to the Cross would they have created their own military divisions and another national symbol, probably a Christian cross, as the Bretons did? Had Welsh knights gone to Jerusalem, would the Cross of St David (a golden cross on a black field) be our sole national flag and the Red Dragon a rather obscure but high-scoring fact in a pub quiz night?

By the time Edward I's men killed Llywelyn ap Gruffudd, the last Prince of Wales, at Cilmeri near Builth Wells in 1282, the dragon had solidified its position as a Welsh symbol. The famous lament to Llywelyn by Gruffydd ab yr Ynad Coch describes him as, '*pen dragon, pen draig oedd arnaw*' (pendragon, the head of a dragon was on him).

The image of the Red Dragon as a symbol of Welsh redemption continued. Owain Lawgoch was killed in Mortagne in France by a spy in 1378 as he plotted an alliance with the French to defeat the English. In a poem lamenting Owain's death, Iolo Goch describes how the White Dragon will flee from the Red Dragon.

The great redeemer, of course, is Owain Glyndŵr. He was proclaimed Prince of Wales in 1400 by a parliament of Welsh gentry. Owain adapted Llywelyn the Last's standard – four lions (rampant in Glyndŵr 's case, passant in Llywelyn's). Owain was impressing his lineage with the Royal House of Gwynedd who had united much of Wales.

However, Glyndŵr also made use of the dragon in different ways. On an official document from 1404 his personal seal shows the dragon supporting his shield. A Red Dragon was attached to his helmet (as it was on Llywelyn the Last's).

Glyndŵr's Yellow Dragon?

But Glyndŵr not only used a Red Dragon but famously flew a flag with a golden dragon on a field of white at the siege of Caernarfon in 1402.

So, Glyndŵr, like Uther, held a golden not a Red Dragon – '*vixillum – album cum dracone aureo*'. Should we Welsh fly a golden rather than a Red Dragon?

'No' is the answer.

In a wonderful article in *Y Fflam* in September 1948, D. J. Davies wrote that he believed that the golden and red are in fact the same colour, albeit in different shades.

'*Aureus*', like '*purpureus*' is a continuum of colours which could differ in the eye of the beholder. They are both shades of red and whose description was not confirmed or standardised and could be described

The Owain Glyndŵr flag

differently by different people. The Royal College of Arms to this day do not use standardised Pantone numbers to denote colours. A red is a red in different shades, as was the case centuries ago.

The Welsh poets use terms such as '*eur rut*' (*aur rhudd*) and '*rhuddaur*' – golden red in English. In Layamon's English translation of Geoffrey of Monmouth's '*Historia*', he describes Uther's standard of 'al of reade golde'. The dragon in Welsh has also been described in Welsh as '*tanbaid*' (flaming) – and fire flickers between red and gold in colour.

I wonder, had Uther's two sculpted dragons or the metallic heads of the Roman '*dracones*' pennants been made of copper or brass, whether would they have been described as red in Welsh? After all, in Welsh '*coch*' could include the spectrum from yellow to brown. What is called 'brown sugar' in English can today still be called '*siwgr coch*' (red sugar) in Welsh. Likewise, 'black tea' (tea without milk) can be '*tê coch*'.

For Glyndŵr to fly a 'golden dragon' on a white field would have been contrary to heraldic convention, and also contrary to just plain common sense. Most knights, for obvious reasons of visibility and convention, would have used contrasting colours. Why would Glyndŵr fly a flag which would, from afar, look like a white flag? The flag of Jerusalem, the five-fold golden cross on a white field, is an exception to this rule, presumably because Jerusalem is so holy.

My guess, for what it's worth, is that Glyndŵr and Uther's dragons were closer to what we today would call copper, or orange, rather than to yellow.

Tudor Fusion

The Welsh continued to dream of Welsh freedom with the dragon as the symbol of the Welsh people.

Following the defeat of Glyndŵr's rebellion, the Welsh looked towards the family of Owain Tudur who claimed decent from King Cadwaladr.

Poems by Robin Ddu o Fôn and Lewis Glyn Cothi sing the praise of Owain Tudur and Henry using the Red Dragon as a metaphor for Wales and redeeming Britain for the Welsh.

Henry Tudor was, of course, well aware of the power of the prophesy that the Welsh would eventually reclaim the island of Britain. He used this to gain Welsh support to fight at the Battle of Bosworth in 1485. The poet Lewis Glyn Cothi describes Henry as:

> *A gwas ynghylch maner goch*
> *A ffyrdd uthr ffordd yr aethoch*

> (A servant around the red flag
> And Uther's way was the road you took)

The Welsh flag was one of the three standards presented by Henry at St Paul's Church following his victory. It was described as 'a red firye dragon beaten upon white and green sarcenet' (sarcenet being a soft silk fabric used for ribbons and flags). The flag was referred to

The yellow-breasted Welsh dragon of Henry Tudor

as 'Cadwaladr's Red Dragon' again, invoking the ancient lineage of the Tudors and of Welsh aspiration for the throne at St Stephen's.

The Red Dragon was incorporated into Tudor heraldry, for a time at least. A Red Dragon with yellow breast (maybe a compromise to the conflicting colours of the dragon?) supported Henry's shield. A redder dragon supported Henry VIII's shield, and a golden dragon supported Elizabeth I's shield.

The Green and White
The genius of Henry Tudor seems to have been to marry the Red Dragon with the white and green background.

The tradition of Welsh soldiers wearing white and green livery was an old one – these were the colours worn by Welsh soldiers at the battles of Lewes (1216), Crecy (1346) and Agincourt (1415).

The choice of colours is interesting and one can suppose that they are related to the colouring of the leek, Wales's national symbol. No doubt, the fact that the two colours were comparatively easy and cheap to dye would be a factor, too, in Welsh soldiers choosing their livery.

According to tradition the use of the leek can be traced back to St David. He is associated with the symbol and it is still worn on St David's Day. The legend says he instructed his soldiers to wear leeks in battle against the English so as to recognise one another. But the leek may go back further to pre-Christian time, and could have been a plant revered by the Celtic Druids.

Whether as a nod to Tudor-style livery or pure serendipity, the Welsh national football team played in white and green vertically-halved shirts from 1895 until 1901. The design was revived for Wales's classy away kit in 2012–13, with the right half (heart side) in green and the left in white.

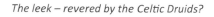

The leek – revered by the Celtic Druids?

The Sleeping Dragon

With the ascent of the Tudors the unbroken dream that the Welsh had held on to since the arrival of the Anglo-Saxons of regaining the throne of Britain (or, at least the biggest part of it) was completed. However, the price to pay for the reconquest of England was that the Welsh had to become English, not the English Welsh.

Whilst the Tudor era confirmed the Red Dragon as a symbol of Welshness, the very success of the Tudors effectively killed Wales as a political nation. Although Henry VII set up a Council of Wales and the Marches which met at Ludlow (in what is now England), his son, Henry VIII, was responsible for the Acts of Wales of 1536 and 1542.

These are sometimes known as the Acts of Union – a rather grand and misleading term coined by O. M. Edwards MP in 1901, the centenary of Ireland's Act of Union with Britain. OM, who, as a schoolchild was caned for speaking Welsh at the time of the Welsh Not, no doubt wanted to give Wales a pumped-up sense of importance within the so-called 'British family of nations'.

The Laws gave individual rights to Welshmen, but no national rights. What was an exercise in tidying up the rule of law and administration for the Tudors had the implicit project of counting Wales as nothing more than thirteen English counties. The law is quite clear: 'That his said Country or Dominion of *Wales* shall be, stand and continue for ever from henceforth incorporated, united and annexed to and with this his Realm of *England*.' (Italics mine.)

And that is why there is no Welsh symbol on the Union Flag (which is also known as the Union Jack). As Wales has been 'incorporated, united and annexed to and with this his Realm of England' it has no more need for a flag than Yorkshire had. 'Our' flag was taken to be England's Cross of St George.

At a time when some 90 per cent of the population spoke only Welsh, the Acts made English the only official language in Wales:

> because that the People of the same Dominion have and do daily use a speche nothing like, ne consonant to the natural Mother Tongue used within this Realm, some rude and ignorant People have made Distinction and Diversity between the King's Subjects of this Realm, and his Subjects of the said Dominion and Principality of *Wales*, whereby great Discord Variance Debate Division Murmur and Sedition hath grown between his said Subjects.

And so the Acts would 'utterly to etirpe alle and singular the sinister usages and customs differing from the same... to an amiable concord and unity', and so:

> From henceforth no person or persons that use the Welsh speech or language shall have or enjoy any office or fees... unless he or they use and excercise the speech or language of English.

The effects of the Acts were slow to be felt, but as

the gentry became anglicised, one by one they stopped sponsoring the Welsh court poets, and Welsh became the language of the 'lower classes'.

With it lingered the smell of Henry VIII's suspicions that the Welsh language and manifestations of Welshness were the cause of 'some rude and ignorant People have made Distinction and Diversity between the King's Subjects of this Realm'.

For many people in authority, and those wishing to have authority since then, Welsh identity, and efforts to promote that identity beyond the St David's Day toast, were seen as suspicious and not quite polite. It's a suspicion and even, at times, hatred of Welsh and Welshness which has dogged the most innocent and polite requests for recognition for Welsh rights and sensibilities since then – including the request for Wales to have its own national flag. And in an effort by the Welsh themselves to appear above suspicion and to become civic Englishmen, they themselves have supressed their own Welshness and language and any thoughts of being a proper country with its own flag.

The story of the Red Dragon flag isn't only about heroes, it's about the cowered too.

In the history of every national flag there is the story of a civil war, armed or political, over what it means to be that nation.

And There Was Nothing Until 1865

For almost 300 years there was barely a mention of a Red Dragon, let alone an idea of a Red Dragon flag.

The Tudor project of incorporating Wales was so successful that Wales barely existed as a nation. Its only distinct institutions were the Great Session Courts and the Welsh language. Although Welsh was still the language of the vast majority of people in Wales, politically the Welsh thought of themselves as English.

Had Scotland not joined a Union with England in 1707 then perhaps Welsh identity would have been completely submerged into English identity – just as it has been in cricket.

Flags, or standards, if used at all, were used by kings and armies and navies – or people who wished to be a king and who had an army and navy. Wales had neither.

Icons but no Flag

It seems peculiar, then, that a nation without a parliament or royal family has a disproportionate number of national symbols. Wales didn't have a flag until the later nineteenth century, but it certainly had no shortage of national icons.

Many symbols were used for Wales and the Welsh before the flag became commonplace.

The leek must surely be one of the oldest continuously-used national motifs in Europe. The daffodil was never used before… but more of that later.

The goat was a popular symbol for Wales and the Welsh. It has been a mascot of the Royal Welch Fusiliers since at least 1775. The goat was still popular as a symbol until the early twentieth century and can be seen adorning paintings, eisteddfodic chairs and the F.A. of Wales. There are many cartoons of goats from the eighteenth century – some humorous; many suggesting the mountainous poverty and backwardness of Wales and the Welsh people.

The Three Feathers were also used and became popular in the eighteenth century. They date back to Edward the Black Prince (1330–1376) and were adopted by Arthur, the son of Henry VII. Flags of the three feathers on a black field were occasionally used to represent Wales in the nineteenth century.

St. David's flag

St David, of course, despite strong anti-Catholic sentiment in Wales, was still celebrated as much as a national icon than Christian saint. There is even a fleeting, tantalising reference to 'David's flag' in the tenth century. '*Armes Prydain Fawr*' (the Prophesy of Britain) of around 930 AD, a popular poem in the Book of Taliesin, prophesied that in the future, when all might seem lost, the Welsh people would unite behind the standard of David to defeat the English: '*A lluman glân Dewi a ddyrchafant*' ('And they will raise the pure banner of Dewi'). '*Lluman*' is an old Welsh word for banner, which in modern Welsh has been revived as '*llumanwr*', the word for linesman in football and rugby matches. It's not clear if the scribe had an actual flag in mind or if it was a metaphorical description. However, '*Lluman Dewi*' wasn't forgotten and makes an appearance in the eighteenth century.

St David's Day was celebrated and became quite fashionable, even within the Hanoverian Court in the eighteenth century.

The London Welsh society, the Society of Ancient Britons, on their St David's Day celebration invitation of 1773 does not feature a dragon. It includes the three feathers of the Prince of Wales and above it the cross of St David – what seems a yellow cross on a black background.

The first official recognition in the modern age of the Red Dragon happens at the very beginning of the nineteenth century, when a Royal Badge of Wales was given. It was defined as the Red Dragon rampant on a green mound and white field.

The Society of Ancient Britons celebrate St. David's Day without a Welsh dragon; by permission of the NLW

There is much disagreement about when this happened. Most recent publications say the badge was given in 1807; others say 1801.

However, I'm thankful to John Petrie, Rouge Croix Pursuivant at the Royal College of Arms in London, for searching their archives to put this matter to rest. Their archives show that the Royal Badge of Wales was recorded on 5 November 1800 by Royal Warrant.

This was, no doubt, as part of the whole reorganisation for the union between Ireland and the UK which came into being on 1 January 1801. Did an early historian believe that the Royal Badge came into practice in the New Year of 1801 with the union with Ireland? To complicate matters, did another later historian mistake the final '1', maybe written with a tail in the continental style, for a '7' and write down 1807? Who knows.

From 1800 there is barely a mention of the Red Dragon, until 25 May 1865 when, as if a shooting star, it appears on the ship *Mimosa*, which took the first settlers to the new Welsh colony in Patagonia, Argentina.

The New Wales

Many books about the Welsh flag will jump straight from the Royal Badge to mention some agitation for the flag in the 1950s culminating in official status in 1959. But this is to totally overlook 150 years, the most interesting part of the history of the Welsh Dragon flag. It ignores the noble efforts of Welsh people to have their national identity recognised and respected. It's the story of the majesty of campaigning, petitioning … and sometimes, even, 'stop pussyfooting and take down the Union Flag'.

Paleo-Dragon

Wales limped into the nineteenth century as part of a United Kingdom in which it wasn't recognised. Despite the Union Flag being redesigned in 1801 to include the red saltire cross of St Patrick, the Welsh were content to be a part of England and be represented by the Cross of St George.

This is what makes the appearance of the Red Dragon flag, fully formed, on the *Mimosa* as she embarked in 1865 for the new Welsh colony in Patagonia, all the more surprising.

There is no mention before that of any Welsh Red Dragon flag being flown before then and none after that for thirty years.

Why was it that no Welshman thought of flying a distinctive Welsh flag before 1865?

How was it that even Iolo Morganwg, 'Mad Ned' to his friends and foe alike, wasn't even mad enough to design a flag? This was the man who invented the druidic Gorsedd of the Bards and its own alphabet; who would have sailed to America in search of the 'lost' Welsh Indians had he not been too ill. He was immersed in Arthurian mythology … but didn't think of creating a Welsh flag with Arthur's dragon.

It may be difficult for people today to understand that at a time when Wales was almost totally a Welsh speaking country, the people lacked a sense of political nationality.

In fact, eighteenth- and nineteenth-century Wales was very much like Africa today. Here we have a governing class who, are in true Tudor principle, ethnically African but civically English and Anglophone. English (or French) is the language of governance in Africa despite the fact that it is the mother tongue of only a tiny minority of the people governed. The parallels with nineteenth-century Wales are clear, and unless the Africans change this situation then their languages will follow the same route and decline as Welsh.

And like African peoples today, the idea of a flag to represent Wales never seemed to have occurred to the Welsh people. The Welsh saw themselves as some kind of tribe, like the Zulu of South Africa or Bemba of Zambia. They spoke their language and had their customs and maybe symbols but there was no idea of a different flag because to have a national flag is to put on cloth your wish to have some sort of civic national recognition or government. The Welsh had no such concept or wish. And in the same way that the Zulu or Bemba don't fly a national flag today, there wasn't a Welsh one until the late nineteenth century. It was the slow rise in the call for a Welsh parliament, Welsh civic institutions, and language rights, that created the need for a flag.

It's not that the Red Dragon was unknown or unused. It hadn't made the revolutionary transformation from a motif to a flag.

But surely, there must have been some context to the Red Dragon being flown in 1865? And, indeed, we do have tantalising insights into a gradual evolution in Welsh thinking through the flag.

In the March 1822 edition of the *Cambro-Briton* the article again notes that Henry VII 'displayed a red dragon upon a standard of green and white silk at Bosworth'.

The author also points out, in what will become a perennial and tedious complaint of loyal Welshmen, that Wales isn't recognised in the Royal Standard.

Gladys of Harlech; or, The Sacrifice, A Romance of Welsh History was a novel by Louisa Matilda Spooner, published in 1858. It was set at the time of Henry Tudor, and also makes reference to the Red Dragon flag or standard. One of the characters laments: 'Well, Howel, let us hope since we have lived to see the joyful change in the Cwm, that you will also live to see that day when the Red Dragon banner floats once more upon our fortress'.

The novel even describes how the Welsh flag looks: 'In secret, she [Gladys] had worked the Red Dragon banner, upon a ground of green and white silk, in anticipation of the present event.'

So, people were aware that there was, once at least, a distinctive Welsh Red Dragon flag. People even knew how it looked. But this was probably a very small number of people in a very niche interest. Maybe the same kind of niche who would, in the 1980s, have known of the now popular, but then less well-known, Cross of St David.

And there does seem to have been a proto-flag. There was one link between describing the Tudor Banner and reinventing it as a proud flag on the *Mimosa*. There is a missing link.

Mr Davies of Cheltenham and the Missing Link

At the impressive three day '*Gordovigion*' eisteddfod held at Liverpool in June 1840, the Red Dragon crept out of the primeval swamp!

In a four-page supplement in the *Carnarvon and Denbigh Herald* of 27 June 1840 mention is made of a flag. The MC of the eisteddfod:

> then pointed to a silk standard that was placed over the president's chair, on which was painted a red dragon, on a green ground, with white border – this, he said, had been sent to him by Mr Davies of Cheltenham, a true Cambrian, who was always ready to keep up the remembrance of the valour of his, and our, country.

The article then notes 'several patriotic gentlemen' who were campaigning for 'the establishment of an Order of Knighthood for Wales.'

It doesn't seem that the flag was actually flown, but rather draped over the eisteddfod chair. However, this, it seems, is the first time in modern times that someone had the vision and gumption to actually transfer and make the Royal Badge into a flag.

Who was Mr Davies of Cheltenham, this visionary who seems to have made the first practical, logical leap?

Henry Davies of Cheltenham was originally from the Vale of Glamorgan. As a young man he was a keen competitor at local eisteddfodau. By 1840 he was editor of the *Cheltenham Looker On* magazine and was a leading local Conservative. He kept his interest in the eisteddfodau, and although he'd lost his fluency in Welsh, he was one of those who presided over the famous National Eisteddfod in Llangollen in 1858 – the

174 years later, Bryn Terfel accepts the St David's Award

44

Eisteddfod at which the National Anthem, in its original form, 'Glan Rhondda', was submitted.

Mr Davies' flag was a small, subtle change in Welsh life. At the same eisteddfod there is a defence of the Welsh language in the editorial – though, typically of the Welsh, it is far too deferential, even though it foresees by thirty years the British state's policy of the 'Welsh Not'.

The 'Order of Knighthood' to which the report refers was a campaign by the Welsh gentry and middle class for Wales to have, like Scotland and Ireland, its own award, named after St David. It says much about the British state's attitude towards the Welsh that even this timid and polite request by such an utterly royalist subaltern class as the Welsh gentry was not recognised. In 2014, 174 years later, the National Assembly created a St David's Award, though this, too, is careful not to be seen to upstage or challenge the English awards by producing a medal.

It seems nothing came of the flag and there seems to be no mention or use of it again. Was it kept in a cupboard in Liverpool, and did its memory live on? Is it just a coincidence that the proto flag was first shown at this eisteddfod in Liverpool and it was from Liverpool that the *Mimosa* sailed to found the colony twenty-five years later?

New Wales – New Flag!

And so we come to 28 May 1865, when the Red Dragon flag was flown on the *Mimosa* as it carried the first settlers from Liverpool to found the Welsh-speaking colony in Patagonia. This was possibly the first time since the Battle of Bosworth that the Red Dragon had been flown publicly. Should this not be our 'Flag Day'?

Who had the flash of inspiration and courage to place the flag on the mast? My guess is that Lewis Jones was the instigator of the flag. With Michael D. Jones, he was one of the principal architects of the venture to create a colony in Patagonia, where Welsh would be the civic language – the language of education, law and officialdom – when it was banned in Wales.

An unofficial stamp published by Y Lolfa commemorating the landing of the Mimosa at Porth Madryn

Lewis Jones had been the editor of the Welsh language magazine *Y Punch Cymraeg*. He later moved to Liverpool where he helped prepare the way for the colonists. Was Lewis Jones aware of Mr Davies's flag, and did he perhaps see it, hold it and be inspired by it?

As the *Mimosa*'s anchor was hauled in Liverpool dock, the leader of the expedition, Cadfan Gwynedd (Hugh Hughes), hoisted the Red Dragon flag which was duly booed by the English on the quay-side. However, the booing stopped once the Welsh started singing an anthem to the new colony, which was to the tune of 'God Save the Queen'!

A letter by John Jones of Mountain Ash, published in *Seren Cymru* in November 1865, notes that the Red Dragon flag was hoisted when the *Mimosa* called at Rio de Janerio en route to Patagonia.

Lewis Jones recalled seeing the flag on flown on the mast as the *Mimosa* approached the Patagonian landing. It seems that one of his fellow Welshmen mistook the Red Dragon flag for the Danish flag.

In a second letter in *Y Gwladgarwr* newspaper, 16 June 1886, John Jones recounted that an eisteddfod was held during the first Christmas at the colony. Jones notes that at eight o'clock on Christmas morning a Red Dragon flag was hoisted on the hill in Caer Antur (the settlement's first village, today the town of Rawson) where a Gorsedd of the Bards duly proclaimed the opening of the eisteddfod. Following competitions in oratory, poetry recital and singing they retired, stereo-typically, for tea and bara brith.

It is no coincidence that it was the Welsh colony which

was the first to fly a flag. After all, flags were flown by independent states or by revolutionaries who wanted to take power over a state or create a new one. Creating a national flag is a political statement as it proclaims that you wish your people to be a state. It was only the bold and brave project to create a Welsh state 7,000 miles from Wales that allowed the Welsh to dream and to have the freedom to fly their own flag.

From 1865 we can see a polite and subtle jockeying for position for which symbol, if any, would become the national flag. A report from the National Eisteddfod held in Aberystwyth that year describes a huge Prince of Wales three-feathers flag on a black background, but no Red Dragon, it seems.

The National Eisteddfod in Aberystwyth – with no dragon

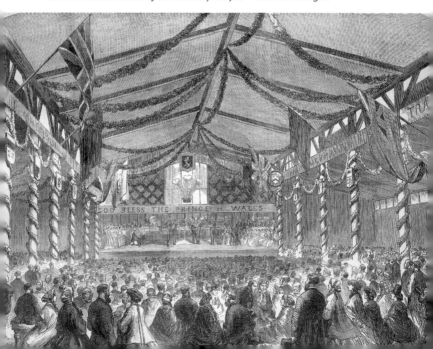

However, perhaps the news, and possible excitement, of the Red Dragon at Liverpool reached Tenby. During a royal visit by the Prince of Wales to the town, *Seren Cymru* (18 August 1865) reported the many signs welcoming the Prince which were in Welsh, as well as '*baner fawr o wyrdd a gwyn (lliwiau Cymru) a'r ddraig goch arni*' ('a large banner of green and white – the colours of Wales – with a red dragon on it') placed in a '*lle amlwg*' (conspicuous location) opposite the royal table at the banquet reception at the Gate House Hotel.

It seems that the Red Dragon on the *Mimosa* may have created a ripple effect. A letter in *Seren Cymru* under the pen name 'Gwirionedd' (truth), published on 9 October 1868, laments the lack of Welsh icons or flags in Cardiff as it welcomed the new Marquis of Bute. The author notes bitterly that there were plenty of English and Scottish icons: 'One would have thought the Welsh had become Scottish, but where were the arms of Wales, a green and white flag of Bosworth field and Cadwaladr's Dragon?'

However, despite an initial flutter of interest and inspiration in the 'new flag', it never quite caught on. It didn't have a political movement behind it. The 7 November 1890 edition of the *Cambrian News* included a report of a public lecture given on 'The Flags of All Nations' in Manchester. The lecturer laments that the Welsh, 'the most loyal citizens of Great Britain' don't have a recognised national flag. One can almost hear the surprise in the *Cambrian News*' reporter's words when he continues, 'according to the lecturer, the Welsh flag was of green and white colour with a red dragon in the centre'

– betraying the fact that the flag was virtually unknown to its readers.

It seems that without the political project of creating a Welsh state and institutions there was no movement for a Welsh national flag. But things were to change, and it's to a man of Gwent, Arlunydd Penygarn, that we should be grateful.

Contemporary comment on Penygarn's struggles in designing the Red Dragon Flag!

The Father of the Red Dragon Flag

If any one person can claim to be the champion of the Red Dragon flag then it must be T. H. Thomas. Given the mind-numbing multitude of Victorian Welshmen who used initials and anglicised patronymic surnames, we'll call him by his well-known and much used bardic name, 'Arlunydd Penygarn' (the Artist of Penygarn).

He was born in 1839, the son of 'Twm Bach Canton', Thomas Thomas from Leckwith in Cardiff. As a boy, Twm Bach earned some extra pennies singing Welsh folk songs in the pubs of Cardiff, but he later became principal of the Baptist College in Pontypool. His son, T. H. Thomas, became an artist and an illustrator in London, before moving to Cardiff where his address, 45 The Walk in central Cardiff, became a busy centre of Welsh life. He was active in many societies: the National Eisteddfod, the Royal Cambrian Academy, the Cardiff Naturalists' Society, and the foundation of the National Museum. His house deserves a plaque in recognition of his tireless campaign for the national flag.

On 23 February 1893 a letter by Penygarn appeared in the *Daily Graphic* calling for recognition for Wales on the new coinage and the following month he received a letter by a I. T. Jacob of Miskin Street in Cardiff, asking him to help promote 'the bearings of Wales on the shield of the UK.' This, it seems, is the beginning of Thomas' crusade to get the Red Dragon onto the Royal Standard and coinage,

THE ROYAL SHIELD OF ARMS OF THE UNITED KINGDOM.
With the RED DRAGON of the Banner of CADWALADR VENDIGAID,
inserted in the Fourth Quarter, for WALES.

Intricate Welsh heraldry now at St Fagans. With the permission of Amgueddfa Cymru / National Museum Wales.

and later the arms of Cardiff and as the national flag.

There then follows a series of letters and petitions and lobbying on this subject from Penygarn.

Thomas' collection at the Museum of Welsh Life at Saint Fagans near Cardiff includes some beautiful intricate diagrams and sketches of Welsh flags and heraldry. They include some musings on two potential alterations to the UK flag – one, a red cross; another a green cross bordering the white background of the Cross of St George. This sketch proposes that either the white cross on red field or on a green field could represent Wales as the Cross of St David and the 'proposed Welsh flag'. There is also a Red Dragon flag on a white field with a Union Jack in the canton (top left corner). We can be eternally grateful that Penygarn never seemed to have any interest nor devoted his considerable energy for the Three Feathers which he saw as an 'imported emblems'.

Despite his own graphic skill and heraldic knowledge, Thomas, in his campaign for a Welsh quarter on the Royal Standard, got the Surrey Herald Extraordinary, C. A. Buckler, to design it properly. The exquisite design places the passant red dragon with blue tongue and claws on the now familiar white and green halved background, in the bottom right corner of the Royal Standard.

Thomas' campaign was supported by the great and the good of Welsh life. However, in an answer at the House of Commons on 12 March 1898 Arthur Balfour announced that Wales would not be included on the Royal Standard. Oh, the irony… Balfour, the man who would later give the Jews a homeland, couldn't give recognition to the

Welsh, who lost 40,000 men in the First World War, and helped 'liberate' Jerusalem.

We've already mentioned the slight felt by 'gallant little Wales' at not being recognised on the royal standard in the 1830s. The Welsh petitioned the government in 1887, 1901, 1910, 1935 and 1945 for the Red Dragon to be included in the royal arms. The Welsh, including Penygarn's campaign, failed because the Garter Knight of Arms told the Home Office that 'there is no more reason to add Wales to the King's style than there would be to add Mercia, Wessex or Northumbria or any other part of England'.

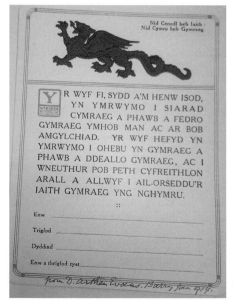

Membership card of the first Welsh Language Society

Is it possible that the disappointment of the royal snub actually made the call for, and use of, a distinctive flag more relevant? Thomas certainly didn't give up.

The artist's campaign gained extra relevance during Queen Victoria's Diamond Jubilee in June 1897, when even the docile Welsh started to feel there was something missing in the lack of a Welsh flag amidst all the Union Jacks that draped the streets.

Penygarn's contribution wasn't only to push for recognition on the royal standard; much more important for his legacy and for the Welsh nation was his promotion of the flag. Penygarn effectively drew the flag into life.

A sketch of Penygarn's Red Dragon flag appeared in the *South Wales Daily News* on 30 March 1897 as an exclusive.

Penygarn became effectively the unofficial Heralder of Wales and authority on the Welsh flag.

A letter from the organisers of the Llanelli Eisteddfod in 1902 were 'anxious to have the design of the Red Dragon'; a R. P. Culley of London wanted the 'correct Welsh Dragon' for his pamphlet. Penygarn received a poignant letter from Hugh D. A. Williams of 4 Spilman Street in Carmarthen. Mr Williams asked Penygarn for information on the badges of Wales as he wishes to commission a stained glass window at St Thomas Church, Ferryside, in memory of his brother, W. A. G. Williams, who was killed at Bothaville fighting for the South Wales Borderers in the Boer War. In October 1902, an enterprising M. F. Sparks, 'importer of Glass and China and Fine Goods', of 11 Queen Street in Cardiff, asks for his advice as he looks to produce cups and

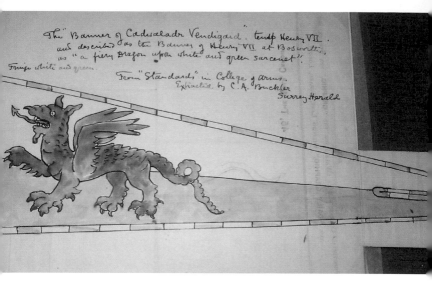

Heraldic Welsh Dragon design by Penygarn. With the permission of Amgueddfa Cymru / National Museum Wales.

saucers to commemorate the addition of the Red Dragon to the royal insignia.

Penygarn designed the National Eisteddfod flag and mace and helped design the Gorsedd stones for the 1899 Cardiff National Eisteddfod, where Patrick Pearse, the Irish Revolutionary, was made a member of the Gorsedd. Penygarn played a prominent part in the Pan-Celtic Gathering in Dublin in August 1901 where his Welsh flag was paraded. A letter by 'Gweryfed' of 29 Tudor Terrace, Merthyr Tydfil, congratulates Penygarn, *'gwelaf mai Draig Goch Cymru oedd ar y blaen yno'*. (I see the Red Dragon was at the front.) This was probably the first time ever the Welsh Red Dragon flag had been seen outside Wales or Patagonia.

Our deliberately underwhelming National Assembly could learn from Penygarn's understanding of Welsh regalia, and give the Senedd some dignity and majesty.

Penygarn was the right man at the right time. His artistic skill and eye ensured that he understood the importance of symbolism and what worked. He had the time, contacts and good name to pursue his passion. These personal attributes coincided with a flowering of Welsh civic institutions which were part of a broader *Cymru Fydd* or Young Wales sentiment, which reflected similar movements in Ireland, Catalonia, the Basque Country, and eastern Europe, such as the Czechs, Slovenes, Slovaks and Baltic nations. It is in the context of these mostly 'non-historic nations' which we should compare the development of the Welsh flag, and in this respect, Wales is at the forefront.

It's impossible to say if the Red Dragon would have become the Welsh flag without Penygarn, but one can say that without him it would have been adopted at least a generation later.

Penygarn's achievements show that one individual can make a difference to a nation's path: that dedication, the gallant trade of letter-writing, hassling and lobbying, can be as heroic as any Dark Ages battle or Middle Ages poem. We all have the opportunity, and responsibility, to make a contribution and write our names in Welsh history.

The Slow Conquest of the Dragon

The years leading to the First World War were the high tide of Liberal patriotic Welsh success. Despite the failure to win self-rule these were the years which saw the foundation of the National Museum, National Library, Welsh Folk Song Society, Welsh Board of Education, and disestablishment of the Anglican Church in Wales.

We've seen how Penygarn revived the idea of the Red Dragon flag, but it was a while before the flag was widely used or known. As late as 1904 the *Barry*

A fine Red Dragon at the Suffragette Procession in London, 1911. With the permission of Amgueddfa Cymru / National Museum Wales.

The design that was embroidered by Rose Mabel Lewis. With the permission of Amgueddfa Cymru / National Museum Wales.

Herald mentions that an Empire Day eisteddfod competition held at Romilly Road Girl's School in Barry, for 'best design for a Welsh flag', was won by M. Christian.

A letter in the *Cambrian News* of June 1901 chastised the people of Bangor during the town's eisteddfod proclamation procession for the lack of a Welsh flag, with only 'Messrs Griffith having a large banner with the Royal arms of Wales challenging the attention of passers-by'.

But others were picking up the baton. The radical Labour politician and MP for Merthyr, Keir Hardy, adopted the red, white and green of the flag as the colours of his campaign literature.

The Cardiff & District Women's Suffrage Society carried a fine Red Dragon flag at the Suffrage Procession in London on 17 June 1911. It was embroided by Rose Mabel Lewis of Greenmeadow, Tongwynlais who was Chair of the Cardiff & District Women's Suffrage Society. Beneath the dragon were the words, '*Tros Ryddid*' (for freedom), written in the style of Iolo Morganwg's invented Bardic script. She proudly walked in front of her banner in the procession, and the dragon attracted a lot of attention. One group of onlookers greeted her, or the flag, with 'here comes the Devil'!

After a letter complaining that only Messrs Griffiths shop on Bangor's High St flew a 'large banner with the Royal arms of Wales' as part of the proclamation of the 1901 Eisteddfod (most flew the Union Jack), even Bangor had a change of heart by 1903, 'the Welsh flag being greatly in evidence' in the High Street for General Baden-Powell's visit to the town in September of that year.

The slow adoption of the flag was caused by some quite mundane issues.

In a less visual age, with no colour film and little colour publishing, the flag was rarely seen. And once the public were aware of it, how or who would produce such a flag? It's also one thing to reproduce a tricolour flag, or even draw a Union Jack, but drawing a Red Dragon which doesn't look like an electrocuted cat is a job only for the most talented of artists or seamstress.

To confuse matters, there were several different versions of the Red Dragon flag flying, as was evident at the Investiture of the Prince of Wales in 1911, which flew a medieval-looking design.

Even if a shopkeeper or individual wanted to fly the flag, where could they buy it from?

What was needed was a big colourful event to give the Red Dragon flag status as the emblem of Wales. On the eve of the Great War, two such events happened to help confirm that in a land of many national emblems and motifs, only the Red Dragon was the flag of Wales. They also helped to make sure that Welsh flags would be made, and could be bought.

Blockbusters!

Both these two big events were held in Cardiff. Between 26 July and 7 August 1909 an extravaganza called 'The Pageant of Wales' appeared in the grounds of Cardiff Castle. The pageant was a Hollywood-esque spectacle recalling the history of Wales and her heroes. Leading figures in Welsh public life (incongruously) acted and dressed up as Llywelyn the Great or Owain Glyndŵr. The Marquis of Bute's wife was Dame Wales.

The Pageant was the brainchild of Captain Arthur Owen Vaughan, more commonly known by his bardic name, Owen Rhoscomyl. It was the apex of the confident, optimistic imperial British Welsh Liberal Wales. It included a cast of 5,000 and was performed twenty-five times to crowds totalling almost 200,000. Huge posters were made, as were stamps depicting an Art Nouveau

A prominent Welsh Dragon on the National Pageant programme, 1909

National Pageant of
WALES
to be held at CARDIFF
from July 26th
to August 7th
Inclusive
JMS

Welsh maiden with her hand resting on a large white shield picturing a rampant Red Dragon. Dame Wales wore a long white medieval-style frock with the Red Dragon emblazoned on it, made by Howells, Cardiff's famous department store. If anyone in Cardiff, or Wales, was unsure what was the pre-eminent symbol of Wales, then the Pageant of Wales dispelled that uncertainty.

Although the Pageant of Wales wasn't a financial success it succeeded in promoting and popularising Welsh history, and there is probably a direct link with the next big blockbuster for Cardiff.

On 15 June 1910 the *Terra Nova* set sail from Cardiff for the Antarctic. On it were the members of Captain Scott's ill-fated expedition, aiming to be the first to reach the South Pole. Cardiff won the privilege to be Scott's departure location after some serious lobbying by Cardiff's industrial and political class. On the ship flew a large Red Dragon flag, which measured some 4 metres x 2 metres.

The flag was once again made by Howells department store in Cardiff. It has the familiar white and green background, but incongruously the Dragon is rampant rather than passant. Perhaps the seamstresses at Howells simply amended the design for the rampant Dragon on the Dame Wales dress. The flag was flown on St David's Day in the Antarctic in 1911 and 1912 and flew on the *Terra Nova* when she returned to Cardiff in June 1913 – though, as the *Western Mail* noted, it looked somewhat smaller. There was a reason for that. When the ship called in at Lyttleton in New Zealand on her return journey,

The Red Dragon flag flown on the Terra Nova *for Captain Scott's expedition to the Antarctic. With the permission of Amgueddfa Cymru / National Museum Wales.*

representatives of the Welsh societies were allowed to cut off pieces of the flag as mementoes.

The Daffodil Blooms

During this period another Welsh motif was born – the daffodil. The flower had absolutely no provenance in Welsh literature or history. It was chosen by Lloyd George for the 1911 Investiture of the Prince of Wales at Caernarfon, after a debate that had been rumbling for several years.

Y Drych newspaper of 1892 noted that the leek, Wales's traditional symbol, was 'not beautiful nor fragrant'. In 1907 Ivor B. John even gave a lecture to the Cymmrodorion Society at Goldsmith's College in London, against the leek and in favour of the daffodil. One can feel his pain as he pleads, 'Welshmen would no longer to the subject to the good-natured banter of their neighbours, who charged them with having no aesthetic taste, no sense of humour, and only a perverted sense of smell'.

Arguments in favour of the daffodil varied. Pro-daffodillers noted that '*Blodeuyn Dewi*' (David's Flower) was one of the Welsh words for daffodil; that it was in bloom during St David's Day and that that the most common Welsh name for Daffodil is '*cennin Pedr*' (St Peter's leek), which at least includes the word 'leek'!

Maybe, simply, Lloyd George like didn't like the leek. Appearance and aesthetics are as important as history in any country's choice of symbols.

No Red Dragon flag for the 1911 Investiture!

The People's Banner

By the beginning of the Great War in 1914 the Red Dragon flag (in different styles) was recognised as the definitive Welsh flag – within Wales, at least.

Patriotism wasn't the only reason for this. Tourism played its part in popularising the flag and making it easier to purchase. The *Daily Post* reported in 1917 that visitors to Wales could purchase little Red Dragon flags, which one assumes, were placed on sandcastles on the beach.

The War Effort also played a part in promoting the flag, or a version of it. Welsh Flag Days were held to raise money for the war effort. The Welsh flags sold were white with a green border and a red dragon in the centre. As a sign of the growing popularity and

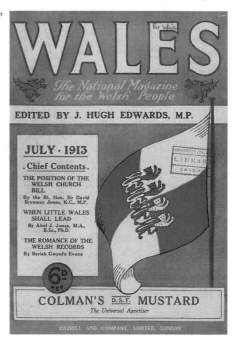

Only little decorative dragons for Wales *magazine, 1913*

affection for the flag, Private Gabriel Ray of Matthew Street, Swansea took a Welsh flag with him to war, and hoped to 'plant it on German soil'.

Hostility or opposition to the flag was rarely open, but would conceal itself in the begrudging and obstructively pedantic attitude of officials. One such example was how the First Commissioner for Works, the MP for St George-in-the-East, Alexander Henderson, refused to allow the Red Dragon to be flown from the Eagle's Tower in Caernarfon castle on St David's Day in 1913 and 1914 as there 'is no Welsh flag'.

His argument was that the Red Dragon was a badge and not a national flag, although there was great support for flying the flag from the tower by a wide cross-section of society. Caernarfon Town Council were in favour, as was Mr Ormsby-Gore, the Conservative MP for nearby Denbigh.

One can well imagine this obstructive attitude within officialdom gave the lead to other officials to hamper attempts to fly the flag on official buildings. The spirit of Edward I still lived at Caernarfon castle!

Following the war the flag became more prominent and acceptable. A heraldic-type flag can be seen in a film of Lloyd George from about 1918 in Cricieth with the equally archaic spelling of 'croeso' as 'croesaw'. By 1927 it seems the modern flag had been accepted by a consensus of Welsh public opinion. A Pathé film from 1927 shows passengers on the Canadian ship *Scythian* arrive for the National Eisteddfod with a magnificent flag in the correct design.

The change in sentiment is belatedly reflected in the vexillogical books (books about flags). E. H. Baxter's 1934 *National Flags* included an entry which describes the modern design, as does Cumberland Clarks *The Flags of Britain*. And it appears in the 1939 edition of *Flags of the World*.

Baxter's *National Flags* notes 'On St David's Day the Welsh flag is flown with the Union Flag on certain official buildings.' The year of publication is significant because of what had happened two years earlier.

The Flag Battle for Eagle's Tower

Caernarfon's relationship with the development of the Red Dragon flag is an important one. Despite official protest in favour of flying the Red Dragon on Caernarfon castle, the polite, deferential Welsh people accepted the verdict not to fly it.

Thankfully, twenty years later, a new generation was not so servile.

The Welsh National Party, Plaid Cymru, was formed in 1925, inspired by Irish self-government and also in reaction to the imperialist carnage of the Great War. Plaid Cymru was small, not much more than a pressure group, and it went against the grain of almost 2,000 years of Welsh aspiration to regain the crown in London. It was this radical break with Welsh deference to London which gave its members the freedom and strength to challenge the primacy of the Union Jack in Wales and make sure the Red Dragon became the recognised flag.

In 1931 the party's new Secretary, J. E. Jones, noticed that only the Union Jack flew on Caernarfon castle on St David's Day. He duly wrote a polite letter to his MP, the former Prime Minister, David Lloyd George, who forwarded it on to Mr Ormsby Gore, First Minister for Works. Ormsby-Gore turned down the modest request to fly the Red Dragon flag. Appropriately enough, he was to be made Colonial Secretary a few years later. And, yes, this is the same Ormsby-Gore who in 1914 was vocal in his support of the Welsh flag, and *against* the then Minister for Works!

This was the response which J. E. Jones had expected. With three others he refused to take the Westminster lies lying down. On the morning of St David's Day, J. E. Jones and three others: E. V. Stanley Jones, a young Caernarfon solicitor; W. R. P. George, a solicitor, and nephew of David Lloyd George; and Wil Roberts, a civil servant, entered the castle. They went up the Eagle's Tower, lowered the Union Jack, hoisted a very large Red Dragon and began to sing '*Hen Wlad fy Nhadau*', at which point the people below began to cheer.

The police eventually arrived and although their names were given, they were set free and no action taken against them. The Union Jack was hoisted up again. But that wasn't the end.

During the afternoon, without the knowledge of the morning's protesters, some twenty students from Bangor came to Caernarfon under the leadership of R. E. Jones. The Union Jack was again lowered and Red Dragon raised. Again the police were called but this time one of the students had the foresight to hide the Union Jack beneath his clothes. Unsuccessful efforts were made later

in the day to burn the imperial flag, but when that failed the protesters contented themselves with cutting up the flag, the symbol of the state's arrogance towards Welsh nationality. They kept the pieces as mementoes.

Surprisingly enough, a year later, shortly before St David's Day in 1933, all the lies about protocol were not seen as a problem. It was announced that the Red Dragon would be hoisted side by side with the Union Jack on

The Red Dragon flies from Caernarfon Castle today

two occasions during the year: St David's Day and the monarch's birthday.

Lloyd George, after twenty years of inactivity as MP on the matter, jumped on the bandwagon. He insisted on appearing in Caernarfon castle to make a show of raising the flag, and spouted the usual waffle, platitude and patronising remarks about Welshness which British politicians still give at these occasions.

Following this success, Plaid Cymru members pressed other local authorities to fly the flag.

It goes to show that the Westminster establishment and her subalterns will readily hide behind supposed protocol or cost to obstruct Welsh national ambitions. It shows that direct action works and respect has to be earned – not politely begged for, Oliver Twist-style.

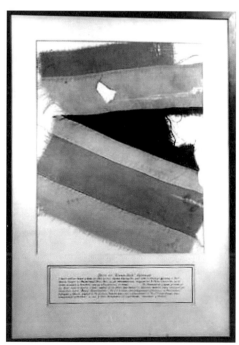

The remains of the Union Jack flown from the Eagle Tower

Official Flag

The protest at Eagle's Tower caused great interest across Wales and beyond. As well as supporters, there was the usual Welsh cringe from Welsh people embarrassed by the event. As we said, the battle for a national flag always includes an element of civil war. The flag now held an element of heroism to it too. That's a vital component if any flag is to have popular sentiment.

It's no coincidence, then, that flag books after 1933 recognise the Red Dragon and include it in all editions.

By the 1950s the flag was widely accepted by the public but official use was still begrudging. The old attitude of the Minister for Works and Henry VIII prevailed; that it was somehow not quite a proper grown-up flag, and perhaps also because it was 'too Welsh' or 'sinister usage'. Many older readers will remember that the flag was rarely seen on public buildings until the late 1950s and its use in that period seemed seems confined mostly to Welsh-language or specifically Welsh events, such as the eisteddfod or *Urdd* youth movement.

However, change was in the air. Again a pageant and big event played their part.

Cardiff was proclaimed capital of Wales in 1955 and in 1958 she hosted the Empire Games. The Games, like all sporting occasions, were an ideal way to propagate the flag, especially through the new medium of film. To complement the Empire Games (subsequently renamed the Commonwealth Games), a series of events, shows and games were held under the banner of *Gŵyl Cymru* (The Festival of Wales). A Pathé film shows a 2-mile long procession, including a 7-metre dragon, passing City Hall in Cardiff. The procession is bedecked with Red Dragon flags in a way which would have been unimaginable a generation earlier.

The first use of the Red Dragon flag in a Wales football programme was on the programme for the Wales v Yugoslavia game in 1953… in Belgrade. Welsh programmes up to that date used various, unstandardised dragon designs, and after 1951 the newly designed beautiful FAW crest was used. The programme for the Yugoslav game played on 21 May 1953 has a hand-drawn, correct, Red Dragon flag, one presumes copied from a book.

Wales v. Yugoslavia football programme, 1953

Politically, some of the anti-colonial sentiment sweeping across the empire was found in Wales as more people wanted some political recognition of Wales as a nation. A cross-party 'Parliament for Wales' campaign was launched in 1950 and active until 1956 when a petition of 250,000 names was presented to Parliament. There were growing calls for a Welsh Secretary of State at the very least. In 1956 a campaign was launched to save the Tryweryn valley near Bala from being drowned to create a reservoir for Liverpool.

But what most people in Wales today will not realise is that the flag mostly flown at those events was not recognised as Wales' official flag. There were two Welsh flags – the popular one we know today and flown at these protests and events, and a now-forgotten official one.

Yes, in 1953 Wales was presented with an official flag – but it was not the familiar Red Dragon. No, it was a rather scrawny red dragon within a belt around it, bearing the motto, '*Y ddraig Goch ddyry gychwyn*', with a representation of the crown on top. It was set on the familiar white and green background.

The flag was the flag of the nascent Welsh Office – what was then the Ministry for Housing, Local Authority and Welsh Affairs. It was a flag designed deliberately to belittle Wales and inspire no sense of pride or ambition. It was essentially, like the Three Feathers flag, a British version of the old Soviet satellite flags for its republics; a kind of Wales-SSR flag; a Welsh flag that wasn't Welsh.

The Prime Minister, Winston Churchill, despised the badge's design. According to Cabinet minutes from

'Odious' official design created in 1953

1953 he called it an 'odious design expressing nothing but spite, malice, ill-will and monstrosity. Words (Red Dragon takes the lead) are untrue and unduly flattering to Bevan'. (It should be noted that Aneurin Bevan, the famous Labour MP, was not, in any way, a Welsh nationalist).

Churchill wasn't the only one who disliked the flag. Lord Elystan Morgan, then a young trainee lawyer in Ceredigion, a Plaid Cymru member and later a Labour MP, was embarrassed at seeing the flag. He recalled that people refused to fly it and some called it a 'one-balled lamb'.

The sexual reference to the flag wasn't out of context either. Unknown to the Queen, the motto, '*y ddraig goch ddyry gychwyn*' (which is also used on the crest of Cardiff) is a very unfortunate one. Rather than being 'unduly flattering', as Churchill thought, it is in fact the first line of a couplet by Deio ab Ieuan Ddu (1450–1480) in celebration of a bull fornicating. The second line is '*ar ucha'r llall ar ochr llwyn*' (above the other, next to a hedge). The '*ddraig goch*', then, was but a name for a well-endowed bull who only 'took the lead' as far as fathering a new herd went!

Although it was the flag that we recognise that was flown by the public, official buildings were told to fly the 'Welsh Office' flag – it was The First Minister of Works revenge.

Again, it was up to Caernarfon to save Welsh pride.

The National Eisteddfod proclamation ceremony is held a year before it visits the host town. In July 1958 preparations were made for the proclamation for the Caernarfon Eisteddfod of 1959 which were to be held within the historic walls of Caernarfon castle. Cynan, the registrar of the Gorsedd of Bards, failed to get confirmation that the popularly-used Red Dragon would be flown on the day of the proclamation. He was adamantly against the Welsh Office flag, which he believed was too 'limp', not to say too undignified and laughable, to be the national flag.

Cynan was no nationalist, anti-establishment figure – he was, after all, the official government censor for Welsh language plays. He would have had in mind an incident at the Pwllheli Eisteddfod in 1955, when activists took down the Union Jack from the top of the Pavilion, and how the Union Jack had been removed from Caernarfon castle in 1932.

It was decided the only flag the Gorsedd would recognise was the familiar Red Dragon design. The Gorsedd called on institutions and public bodies across Wales to follow their lead, and received unanimous support (with the exception of Newport Council). This popular support for the flag, and backing from such conservative bodies as the local councils of Wales, sent a clear message to the government.

On 23 February 1959 the Conservative MP for Barry, Raymond Gower, tabled a question on the Welsh flag. In response, Henry Brook, Conservative MP and Minister for Housing and Local Government and Welsh Affairs, announced in March 1959 that the Queen had given her seal of approval to the people's Red Dragon.

The unloved Welsh Office flag was binned and has been forgotten.

After hundreds of years in development and decades in use, the traditional Red Dragon flag was officially recognised.

Thanks to the Romanised Brythons, Urther Pendragon, Cadwaladr Fendigaid, Glyndŵr, Harri Tudor, Mr Davies of Cheltenham, the Patagonian pioneers, Arlunydd Penygarn, the rebels of 1932 and Cynan, and to all the letter-writers and the members of the awkward squad who fought for Welsh dignity, the Red Dragon was officially recognised by the Queen – because the Welsh people willed it and campaigned for it, and flew it without her and her officious officials' permission.

The Red Dragon Flag Today

You can't walk anywhere in Wales without bumping into a Dragon! Since the growth of Welsh nationalism in the 1960s, the flag is flown from government and council buildings and offices, and at sporting events. Since the beginning of the century it has also become quite fashionable and acceptable to fly the flag outside private homes and schools.

There are still occasionally calls for the Red Dragon, or a representation of Wales, to be placed on the Union Jack. Ian Lucas, Labour MP for Wrexham, made such a call in 2007. Considering the generations of fruitless calls for the Red Dragon to be included in the Royal Standard, one can hardly think of a more pointless and ultimately unsuccessful campaign as to deface the iconic Union Flag with a Welsh sop.

Likewise, despite the strong affection by the Welsh nation for the Red Dragon flag, there are still occasional minority statements that the Dragon is a satanic symbol. In 2007 a Pentecostal minister and self elected leader of the Welsh Christian Party, George Hargreave, called it 'the evil symbol of the devil.' The man who'd previously made a fortune as a songwriter and producer of big gay disco hit anthems such as 'So Macho' and 'Cruising' added, "This is the very symbol of the devil described in the Book of Revelation 12:3", and called for changing the flag.

Despite periodic calls by 'marketing experts' to change the dragon for a less clichéd image, any country or brand

would give their right arm and serious money to own such a distinctive and inspirational motif and flag.

The Red Dragon flown at Portmeirion

Contentious Flag

 The Red Dragon is still a flag of contention. In 2009, following a campaign lead by Janet Ryder, Plaid Cymru AM, against the then Labour government, it was officially allowed to be placed on the new car registration plates. The variation of the flag flown on the plates vary as the design is the personal whim of garage owners and some are badly proportioned.

In 2015, in an effort to "unite the country" (the UK, not Wales), the UK government decided the Union Jack would be printed on all new driving licenses, despite calls to include the Red Dragon in Wales and Saltire in Scotland. Alun Cairns, Conservative MP for the Vale of Glamorgan and Deputy Minister in the Wales Office, was against the call for the Red Dragon on grounds of "costs" - even though Northern Ireland is exempt from showing the Union Jack. Cairns's attitude was sad and ironic considering it was his Conservative predecessor from the same electoral seat, Raymond Gower, who called for the Red Dragon flag to be officially recognised in 1959. It seems personal political ambition, begrudging spirit and the same excuses of the old Ministry of Works live on in the actions of the Wales Office.

Like the National Anthem, the Red Dragon flag was chosen by the Welsh nation. It was not given to us; it was not invented by a panel; we did not have a parliament or monarchy to decree our flag. We had to struggle against officialdom, patronising excuses and no small element of suspicion of any Welsh pride, to have it made official.

Red Dragon Design

A cursory look at the Red Dragon flag, or rather, flags, will show a wide range of designs and dragons.

Many early designs show a rather reptilian dragon. The tail can include a serpent-like double knot and is frequently turned facing downwards – a style ridiculed once in the *Western Mail* newspaper.

The colouring of the Red Dragon flag breaks the 'rules of tincture' which were laid down, ironically, by the Welshman Humphrey Lhuyd in 1568. Lhuyd (an early, archaic way of spelling Llwyd) was a man of many talents and part of an exceptional generation of Welsh Humanists. He was MP for East Grinstead and later Denbigh. He promoted an Act allowing the translation of the Bible into Welsh, and at Antwerp collaborated with the famous map maker Ortelius. He was later given a stipend from the Crown to create the first printed map of Wales – the '*Cambriae Typus*'. He was also the first to suggest that Prince Madog 'discovered' America in the twelfth century.

In 1568 he laid out the first rule of heraldic design as the rule of tincture. That is, 'metal should not be put on metal, nor colour on colour'. This means that *or* and *argent* (gold and silver, which are represented by yellow and white) may not be placed on each other; nor may any of the *colours* such as *azure* (blue), *gules* (red) *sable* (black) *vert* (green) and *purpure* (purple) be placed on another colour. To do so disguises the design and makes it less easy to recognise.

The bottom half of the Red Dragon on the green background evidently breaks this rule, as do the Bangladeshi, Albanian and Basque flags.

Official Standardisation

The preparation for the Investiture of Charles Windsor as Prince of Wales in Caernarfon in 1969 spurred the authorities on to issue some guidelines. Again, maybe the memory of previous scandals at Caernarfon castle would have led the nervousness: there should be no risk of misunderstanding or misrepresention of the flag. With the rise of Welsh nationalism in the 1960s, attitudes in Wales had changed significantly by 1969, and the monarchy would have wanted to avoid anything which could be seen as a slight or belittlement of Welsh nationality.

MrFlag®, Wales's oldest flag makers, were sent a design by the Welsh Office in 1969. There is also a similar version but with a thin black fimbriation (a fringed margin) used by the Flag Institute.

The College of Arms in London have no Pantone numbers for their colours, so red or green can vary in shade. That may have been acceptable in the Middle Ages, but not in the age of mass-produced flags. The Flag Institute art for the Dragon used Red 032 and Green 354, and was created by Dr William Crampton in the early 1980s, but the current version uses Red 186 and Green 354, though MrFlag® use Red 186 and Green 355.

From an aesthetic point of view, the dark green matches the lush green of the Welsh landscape – giving the impression the flag is of this land.

Other Flags of Wales

St David's Flag

The golden cross on a black field flag was virtually unknown in Wales until the late 1990s. Its sudden rise in popularity may be because the Red Dragon, being so ubiquitous, meant that people wanted another alternative flag, and was also popularised at the St David's Day parade, which began in Cardiff in 1999. The flag was further popularised when it was adopted by Cardiff City FC in 2002.

Although *Armes Prydain* from the tenth century mentions '*lluman Dewi*' (David's flag) this may have been a more figurative flag than an actual banner. As we've seen above, representations of the flag were made in the nineteeth century, and it was also represented badge of the 38th Welsh Division in World War Two.

Church in Wales Flag

With the disestablishment of the Anglican Church in Wales in 1922, the ancient dream of an independent Welsh church, for which Gerald of Wales had campaigned in the twelfth century, was achieved.

There were various versions or claims for different St David's flags, including the now familiar golden cross on a black field. For some reason, some took it upon themselves to reverse these colours, and a black cross on a yellow field flag was flown in 'many churches from about

1936 until the end of 1954', according to the Flags of the World.

On 9 December 1954, following negotiations with the College of Arms, the Church in Wales adopted a new flag. It is white with a blue cross throughout, charged in the centre with a Celtic Cross in gold.

Owain Glyndŵr Flag

Like the St David's flag, the Glyndŵr flag came into popularity at the time of the foundation of the National Assembly in 1997, and then the 600th anniversary celebrations of the proclamation of Glyndŵr as Prince of Wales in 1400. The success of the flag could be an expression of a more radical Welshness which the Red Dragon, being so widespread, does not now represent.

Glyndŵr's arms are based on those of Llywelyn ap Gruffydd (the Last Prince of Wales) who was killed in 1282. Llywelyn's arms were sometimes used at the beginning of the twentieth century.

Glyndŵr's flag, as a standard, should be flown in a square-shaped banner, rather than the 3:5 proportions of regular flags. The 3:5 gives a rather inelegant and elongated look to the rampant lions. From an aesthetic point of view Llywelyn's lions passant on a square banner would look better. In fact, had the 700th anniversary of Llywelyn's death in 1982 captured the public's imagination as much as Glyndŵr's 600th anniversary in 2000, maybe Llywelyn's standard would be the alternative flag. Llywelyn's anniversary came too early for Wales.

Chartists' Flag

A surprisingly under-used flag – blue, white and green horizontal tricolour – was flown by the Chartists as they marched on Newport on 4 November 1839, where some twenty-two were killed outside the Westgate Hotel in the town.

The colours may seem 'un-Welsh' to modern eyes, and some versions of the Chartist flag, and later the Suffragette flag, have purple rather than blue. According to David B. Lawrence, the flag was designed by William Hughes, a radical lawyer from Carmarthen, who was later to translate *Uncle Tom's Cabin* into Welsh. Hughes, who was also known by his bardic name, Cadvan (not to be confused with Cadfan who sailed to Patagonia). He would have been familiar with colours of the three orders of the Gorsedd of Bards, invented by Iolo Morganwg. Iolo's Gorsedd were to be republican Freemasons. The first ceremony to incorporate the eisteddfod with the Gorsedd was held at the Ivy Bush Hotel in Carmarthen in 1819, and Cadvan would no doubt have been aware of it.

Incredibly, it seems that Cadvan's son was William Williams, whom we mentioned above. He was the soldier killed in action in the Boer War. It was his brother, Hugh D. A. Williams, who requested from Penygarn details of Welsh symbols to create a stained-glass window in his brother's memory.

Alternative Flags

Republican Flag
A very rarely flown Welsh Republican tricolour exists. It is a green, red and white vertical tricolour. It occasionally has a black star in the white third, in remembrance of Welsh who have died for Wales.

Y Trilliw
In an article in *Planet* magazine in December 1998, the author Meic Stephens (not to be confused with Meic Stevens the singer) suggested adopting a tricolour which would be used for state occasions. In the wake and excitement of opening the National Assembly, Stephens believed the Red Dragon reminded him of 'our distant origins and our status, for more than a thousand years, as a "non-historic people"'. It is true that stateless nations have more elaborate and unorthodox flags – a vexillogical version of a colourful folk costume, as opposed to a diplomat's pinstriped suit of the tricolour of independent nation states. His alternative was the '*Trilliw*' of green, white and red vertical tricolour, but to the unusual proportions of 1:1:4.

Maritime Flag

In the light of the fact that the lower half of the Red Dragon flag breaks the rules of tincture and that since 2010 the National Assembly of Wales has competence over the maritime economy, the author proposes a Welsh Maritime Flag.

This Maritime Flag would keep the present design and proportions but with the green field lowered, so that the green is below the soles of the Dragon's claws. From a distance the flag would be easier to see and the green ground would mean it would not be confused with the Japanese Red Sun flag.

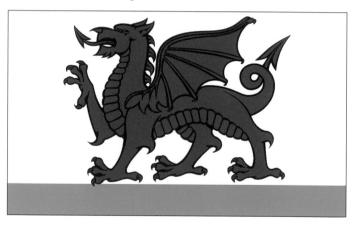

The Issue of the Union Jack in Wales

For many, maybe most Welsh people, the Union Jack is a cold flag; reserved for official buildings and occasions. Since the 2012 London Olympic Games and the rise of Scottish nationalism, there has been a concerted push by the British state media and its agents to popularise it.

For many Welsh people however, the Union Jack is too deeply associated with British imperialism and, at best, a begrudging attitude by its supporters to any meaningful expressions of Welsh identity. It is the flag which embodies the ideology of the Welsh Not. An ideology, which, despite occasional nods to the British 'family of nations', is, at its core, a civic Englishness with a romantic Celtic accent.

Not all supporters of the Union Jack are anti-Welsh by any means, but all anti-Welsh people support the Union Jack. To fly the Union Jack is to hoist up the white flag and surrender Welsh nationality.

Flag Protocol

Protocol and Etiquette

In 2010 the Flag Institute, in consultation with the Flags and Heraldry Committee of the Westminster Parliament, published detailed flag protocol. The publication serves as a useful guide for flying, folding and flag convention. The National Assembly has a protocol on flying the flag which follows this.

However, there is no designed protocol specifically for the Red Dragon itself. The author would suggest that ultimate responsibility for the flying, colouring, design and use of the flag as a national symbol should rest with a House Committee of the National Assembly, under the chairmanship of the Llywydd, the Presiding Officer of the Assembly. A member of the Flag Institute could give evidence and advice to this committee.

Maybe the most basic and important protocol for readers is the one most often broken by ordinary flag wavers. As Welsh people read from left to right the Red Dragon should also follow this convention and face left (from the viewer's vantage). To do otherwise would, for the Western eye, mean to see the Dragon's backside first!

The author would suggest there should never be any law against defacing or burning the Red Dragon flag. The flag is a symbol. People, Welsh people included, have the right to disagree for what they may believe it stands for.

Flag Day

There is no designated Flag Day for the Red Dragon.

The author would propose 28 May, which was the day the flag was hoisted on board the *Mimosa* ship on its voyage to Patagonia in 1865. This was the first known and dated occasion when the flag was flown by Welsh people as a symbol of a Welsh national identity.

The author would like to thank the following for their suggestions and guidance:

Marion Löffler (finding the reference to the Gordovigion Eisteddfod in Liverpool)
Jane Aaron (on early nineteenth-century literature)
Rhys Kaminski-Jones (for information on the coat of arms of the Society of Ancient Britons)
Elen Phillips, Museum of Welsh Life, Saint Fagans, Cardiff
Charles Ashburner, CE 'Mr Flag©', Swansea
John Petrie, Rouge Croix Pursuivant, College of Arms
Peter Owens, Welsh Rugby Union
Prys Morgan
E. Wyn James
Elvey MacDonald
Paul O'Leary
Martin Johnes
Simon Brooks
Gareth Popkins
Huw Walters
Miša Hejna

Also by Siôn T. Jobbins

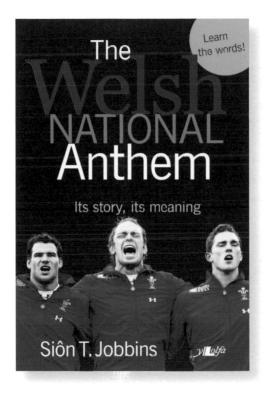

The ful story of the Welsh national anthem – with words!
978-1-84771-650-0
£3.95

The Red Dragon is just one of a wide
range of books of Welsh interest
published by Y Lolfa.
For a full list of books currently in print,
simply surf into our website where you
can browse and order on-line, and also
order a paper catalogue.

www.ylolfa.com
TALYBONT CEREDIGION CYMRU SY24 5AP
e-mail ylolfa@ylolfa.com
phone (01970) 832 304
fax 832 782